Why Do We Wear?

High-Style Clothes
through History

by
Fiona MacDonald

GARETH**STEVENS**
GS
PUBLISHING
Member of the WRC Media Family of Companies

Please visit our Web site at: www.garethstevens.com
For a free color catalog describing Gareth Stevens Publishing's
list of high-quality books and multimedia programs, call
1-800-542-2595 (USA) or 1-800-387-3178 (Canada).
Gareth Stevens Publishing's fax: (414) 332-3567.

Library of Congress Cataloging-in-Publication Data

McDonald, Fiona, 1942-
   High-style clothing through history / by Fiona McDonald.
     p. cm. — (Why do we wear?)
   Includes index.
   ISBN-10: 0-8368-6855-2 — ISBN-13: 978-0-8368-6855-5 (lib. bdg.)
   1. Fashion—History. 2. Fashion designers—History. 3. Lifestyles.
  4. Style (Philosophy) I. Title.
   TT507.M383 2006
   391.009—dc22   2006019081

This North American edition first published in 2007 by
Gareth Stevens Publishing
A Member of the WRC Media Family of Companies
330 West Olive Street, Suite 100
Milwaukee, Wisconsin 53212 USA

This edition copyright © 2007 by Gareth Stevens, Inc. Original edition copyright © 2006
by ticktock Entertainment Ltd. First published in Great Britain by ticktock Media Ltd.,
Unit 2 Orchard Business Centre, North Farm Road, Tunbridge Wells, Kent TN2 3XF.

Managing editor: Valerie J. Weber
Gareth Stevens editor: Gini Holland
Gareth Stevens art direction: Tammy West
Gareth Stevens designer: Kami Strunsee

Picture Credits (t=top, b=bottom, l=left, r=right, c=center) Alamy: 23t; Bridgeman Art Library: back cover and
title page, 12-13 all, 14 all, 19 all, 20-21 all, 22 all; CORBIS: 6 all, 7b, 16-17c, 18 all, 26b, 27b; Shutterstock: 28 all,
29b; ticktock Media Image Archive: cover and title page, 4-5 all, 7t, 16t, 23b, 24-25 all, 26t, 27t, 29b; Werner Forman
Archive: 15t, 8-9 all, 10 all, 11 all, 15b; World Religions: 17t, 17b.

Every effort has been made to trace the copyright holders, and we apologize in advance for any unintentional omission.
We would be pleased to insert the appropriate acknowledgements in any subsequent edition of this publication.

Printed in the United States of America

1 2 3 4 5 6 7 8 9 10 09 08 07 06

Table of Contents

Cover: A runway model wears the latest haute couture fashion.

Words that appear in the glossary are printed in
boldface type the first time they occur in the text.

Introduction

Fashion is big business and employs millions of people. Fashion is also deeply personal. By choosing which fashion styles to wear, we can tell other people a lot about ourselves, where we come from, and which groups we identify with.

Trendsetters

Fashion is fresh, exciting, and sometimes strange and experimental. Twice a year, top designers show their latest styles to celebrities, wealthy customers, and journalists. Few of these clothes are ever worn by people outside the fashion or entertainment industries. Instead, they are designed to set new trends — such as short skirts or wide shoulders — that will be copied by manufacturers making mass-market clothes to sell.

New fashions are displayed by supermodels, accompanied by the latest music.

Looking Different or Alike

Being fashionable means looking different from year to year. Trends in clothes, makeup, and hairstyles change rapidly. At the same time, fashion means looking like others. Wearing the same fashions as our friends is one of the most powerful ways of showing which age group or interest group we belong to.

Wedding clothes look alike at this mass wedding for members of the Unification Church in Korea.

Haute Couture

Top fashion (sometimes called **haute couture**) is rare and expensive. For centuries, top fashion clothes have been carefully made by hand to fit each customer, using the finest fabrics and decorations. These beautiful garments are usually made for special occasions, such as parties, weddings, or other ceremonies. Haute couture is extremely expensive, so ordinary people cannot usually afford it. In the past, it was worn by royalty and members of noble families. Today, it is mostly seen on movie stars and other celebrities.

*What does **haute couture** mean?*

Fashion and Finery

Top fashions and other special-occasion clothes are sometimes known as "finery." They make the wearers feel fine — confident, attractive, and secure in the knowledge that they are looking their very best. Finery need not be expensive. Bright, cheerful colors, interesting shapes, eye-catching decorations, wit, flair, or imagination can all create flattering garments that make their wearers feel powerful, good-looking, happy, or relaxed or put them in a party mood.

Introduction

Fancy dress finery is fun!

5

The First High-Style Clothes

Today, we wear clothes to keep us warm, dry, and modestly covered. We wear special, high-style clothes to look our best at special events. The first fashions were probably made to help people look important, and even magical, when they took part in religious rituals and other important ceremonies.

Not Like Others

For many centuries, ceremonial clothes sent out a message that the people wearing them were special. They might have been priests or **shamans** (people who are seen as healers). Their clothes had magic or symbolic meanings, designed to show purity or spiritual power.

A Congolese tribal dancer wearing a traditional costume and mask.

Slow to Change

Early clothes were often slow to change. Historians have suggested two reasons for this. First, before machines and fast methods of transportation were invented, clothes could only be made by hand from local materials. Secondly, in traditional cultures ordinary people had few opportunities to change their occupations, status, or **peer** groups. Their social status, combined with customs or laws, determined which clothes they were allowed to wear.

A South African shaman points to the Sun while wearing a variety of animals skins.

Status Symbols

Early clothes and body ornaments were like modern fashions in some important ways. To show a leader's wealth and status, they were made of valuable materials, such as furs, feathers, amber, ivory, gold, and precious stones. The most costly of these status symbols were exotic — that is, they could not be found locally but had to be imported from far away. As early as about 10,000 B.C., traders traveled vast distances to meet merchants from distant lands at fairs (trading camps) to trade valuable finery and other goods. Walking there and back home might take many months of each year.

Valuable amber beads like these were traded over long distances in the Middle East.

Who said, "We must suffer to be beautiful"?

Marks of Suffering

Special clothes, ornaments, and face paint were also signs of belonging to a place, a family, or a tribe. Other marks of group loyalty included tattoos, body piercing, and **scarification** (raised patterns of scars on the skin). Getting these marks might actually be painful and dangerous or cause permanent harm. Wearers endured the pain because the final look was seen as a symbol of courage, maturity, rank, or beauty. Such marks may have also protected tribal members from being kidnapped by other tribes.

This Maori from New Zealand wears tattoos as a symbol of strength and bravery.

Ancient Egypt and Its Neighbors

A ncient Egyptian civilization lasted for 3,000 years. During that time, clothing styles changed hardly at all among ordinary people. For the rich, however, a few new fashions were created in clothes, wigs, and jewels.

Wonderful Wigs

In ancient Egypt, fashionable people and some top entertainers displayed their status and artistic flair by their choice of jewels and wigs. These were very expensive symbols of **prestige**. The earliest wigs were short and simple. After about 1500 B.C., long wigs became fashionable. Many were decorated with beads and ringlets, which are long, loose curls. After about 300 B.C., natural hair replaced wigs.

Two musicians and a dancer wear wigs to entertain nobles. This drawing is from the Tomb of Nakht, from about 1567 to 1320 B.C.

Longer, Fuller Fashions

Beginning in about 3000 B.C., men and women wrapped lengths of fabric around their bodies to make short skirts or dresses. By 2100 B.C., men's and women's fashions became longer and looser. By about 1500 B.C., important men and women wore long, pleated skirts or gowns made of fine, transparent fabric held in place by belts around the waist. Lengths of cloth were also draped over the shoulders to create wide, airy sleeves. None of these clothes were sewn.

Pharaoh Tutankhamen, who reigned from 1334 to 1325 B.C., is wearing a pleated skirt.

Murex shellfish, used to make dye, were taken from the warm waters of the eastern Mediterranean Sea.

Classic Colors

In Egypt, white was the most fashionable color. Cool, crisp linen (made from flax) — the Egyptians' favorite fabric — was difficult to dye but could be bleached by stretching it out to dry in Egypt's hot midday sun. Among neighboring peoples, deep purple was the most fashionable and expensive color. It was made by rotting murex shellfish in seawater for months or years. This messy, smelly process created a deep purple dye that bonded to wool or to fancy Asian fabrics like imported cotton and **silk**.

Fashions for Burial

In regions like North Africa and neighboring West Asia, where clothing styles changed slowly, fine, fashionable jewelry was an important symbol of wealth and status. Some of the world's best metalworkers lived and worked in Sumer (modern Iraq and Syria), about 2000 B.C. They created fabulous new finery to be worn by the royal family — even when they were buried in splendid tombs underground. These jewels included **diadems** and other hair ornaments made in local Sumerian style.

This jewelry was discovered in the tomb of Queen Pu-Abi of Ur, Sumer's capital city.

Ancient Greece and Rome

A ncient Greek clothes were made of lengths of cloth that were draped, pinned, and tied around the body. They were never sewn. The Greeks created elegant looks by arranging drapes, pleats, and folds to suit their individual figures.

Fine Fabrics

The Greeks were not greatly interested in fashionable clothes. Styles remained much the same for many centuries, but fabrics changed as Greek traders made contact with far-distant lands. The earliest Greek garments, worn about 1200 B.C., were fashioned from stiff, heavy, woolen cloth. By about 800 B.C., Greek weavers were producing lighter, more graceful fabrics, using finely spun local wool and also **linen** from Asia Minor (now Turkey). They also began to produce colored fabrics. After about 500 B.C., women's clothes became finely pleated.

The powerful man (*left*) wears a chiton. The women (*right*) wear colorful, patterned robes.

Simple Styles

Styles for Greek men and women were similar. Older men and powerful younger men, such as government leaders, wore long **chitons** (tunics) as signs of authority. Women wore **peploses**, robes with a double layer of fabric for the **bodice**. Young men chose shorter tunics. Outdoors, everyone wore a **himation**.

The peplos was tied round the waist with ribbon or with an embroidered **girdle**, which is a tied belt.

From their home city of Rome in southern Italy, the Romans conquered a vast empire. It stretched from Germany to North Africa. Many different styles were fashionable in separate parts of the empire at different times.

Roman Power, Roman Style

According to Roman traditions, the city of Rome was founded in 756 B.C. The Romans had to fight for power against an important neighboring people, the Etruscans. The Romans defeated the Etruscans but learned from their advanced technology and elegant art and design. The Etruscans were expert jewelry makers and wore fine clothes based on Greek and West Asian styles. The Romans copied the Etruscans' favorite *tebenna* (semi-circular robe). They called it a **toga**. Over the centuries, the toga came to be seen as the national dress of Rome.

A Tarquinii servant wears a tebenna.

How did wars change Roman hair fashions?

Togas and Tunics

Togas could be worn only by male citizens — not by women or slaves. The most prestigious togas, with purple borders, were worn by senators. At first, togas were worn alone. By 300 B.C., Romans added a long tunic underneath. As the Roman Empire expanded, new styles were imported. In about A.D. 190, the dalmatic robe became fashionable. It came from Dalmatia (now Yugoslavia) and had a high neckline, long sleeves, and sewn side seams.

This statue shows Julius Caesar (died 44 B.C.) wearing a toga.

Medieval Europe

At first, medieval fashions were influenced by Roman robes and by Saxon and Viking designs. By the end of the Middle Ages, fashion had been transformed by luxury fabrics imported from Asia and by tailoring, which involved sewing techniques that helped clothes fit closely.

Flowing Fashions

By the end of the Roman era (about A.D. 500), togas had been replaced by long, loose, all-covering robes for men and women. Women also covered their heads, necks, and shoulders with wide, flowing veils. These fashions looked stately and impressive and were very modest.

A page from a fourteenth century manuscript shows the King and queen of England dressed in flowing robes.

Flowing robes, however, were suitable only for rich, powerful people who did not have to do hard, physical work. Soldiers, servants, and slaves all wore shorter, less roomy tunics.

This eleventh-century Viking silver armband was made in Sweden.

Northern Style

In northern Europe, pagan tribes migrated — and fought — to establish new kingdoms. Each had its own traditions of decoration and design. Vikings from Scandinavia (powerful from about A.D. 800 to 1100) favored massive silver jewelry for men's and women's fashions. Viking men wore jewelry with tunics. Women wore jewelry with long woolen dresses. Both sexes wore long cloaks, and the rich trimmed all these garments with fur or patterned, woven braid.

Teenage King Richard II (*kneeling*), who ruled from 1377 to 1399, wears a robe with heraldic patterns and fashionable trimming.

Royal Robes

After about A.D. 1200, the fashionable clothes and armor worn by medieval warriors, nobles, and kings featured new, **heraldic** designs. These displayed **emblems** and symbols of the wearer's high status or noble ancestry. For battle and when taking part in favorite noble sports such as hunting, young men and warriors wore suits of armor or thigh-length tunics with pants and boots. When attending **formal** ceremonies, noblemen wore ankle-length robes and cloaks.

What were the favorite trimmings for medieval fashions?

Figure Display

Toward the end of the Middle Ages, new ways of tailoring allowed clothes to fit much more closely. Fashions that revealed body shapes became very popular among rich young men and women. Women's clothes featured low, scooped necklines, narrow sleeves, tight waists, and skirts that flared outward from the hips to reach the floor. Fashionable men wore short, tight **doublets** (fitted tunics) with wide shoulders and narrow waists. Men also wore pointed shoes and clinging **hose**, which were separate stockings for each leg, cut and sewn from cloth.

The explorer Sir Walter Raleigh wears a highly tailored outfit.

Asia

For ordinary people in Asia, fashions changed slowly. Most people continued to wear the same simple styles for centuries. Among ruling classes in India and China — Asia's two largest civilizations — rank, occupation, and political changes all influenced fashionable clothing styles.

Dragon Robes, Wide Sleeves

In China, the right to wear different kinds of clothing was controlled by law. Ordinary men and women wore wrap-over jackets and long, baggy pants, but men from the ruling class were allowed to dress in long, heavy robes with wide sleeves. Starting in 1391, Chinese mandarins (royal officials) added large square emblems displaying their rank.

In this portrait by Pere Bouvet, a mandarin woman wears a summer ceremonial costume.

Chinese Influence

Brightly colored kimonos were for young unmarried women only.

Japanese and Korean fashions were often influenced by designs from China. Soon after A.D. 700, traditional Japanese clothes (a short jacket over pants or a skirt) were replaced by a long Chinese-style robe, later known in Japanese as a kimono. For centuries, it was fashionable for Japanese women to wear many layers of thin, fine kimono robes. The edges of the sleeves and necklines were carefully adjusted so layers of contrasting colors could be displayed.

Why were powerful Chinese men's robes decorated with dragons?

This fourteenth-century samurai armor was made for ceremonial occasions.

Warrior Styles

The formal clothes worn by Japanese samurai (high-ranking warriors) also changed according to fashion. After about A.D. 1000, they consisted of kimono-style robes. Later, they included wide, pleated skirt-pants plus a top with big, padded shoulders. Armor worn by samurai warriors became more elaborate at the same time. It shielded the samurai's body with overlapping iron plates or panels of woven bamboo. Samurai protected their heads with helmets topped by wood or metal crests that identified the ruler they fought for. For safety, they hid their faces behind ferocious masks.

Palace Fashions

In India, political change brought new clothing styles. Traditionally, Indian people wore clothes made by wrapping lengths of cloth around the body — **saris** for women and **dhotis** (loin cloths) for men. Muslim Mongol and Mogul emperors, who ruled northern India after about 1300, introduced new tailored garments based on ancient Persian designs. Long, close fitting *jamah* and *farji* (coats) together with *isar* (big pants) became fashionable for men and women at the emperor's court. After about A.D. 1600, women added sewn, instead of wrapped, *ghaghra* skirts and short, tight *choli* (blouses).

This Indonesian woman makes a batik by drawing a design in wax and then dying the cloth. Dye does not color the waxed parts. When the wax is melted off, the design is revealed.

Africa

In many parts of Africa, the traditional fashion was nudity — especially for younger people. According to many ancient local traditions, nudity was a sign of dignity and purity. Adults who wore clothes wore simple coverings. Some rich adults added extra clothes and jewelry.

This man from Algeria wears *etu*, a blue fabric

Fine Fabrics

Most African fashions were made from lengths of cloth draped around the body. African fabrics had been famous since ancient Egyptian times for their bold patterns and bright colors. The fashionable colors were vivid red, yellow, and blue. In Nigeria, blue **etu** (fabric dyed with indigo) was called "the father of all cloths." Other favorite fabrics included **bogolan** (mud cloth) from Mali, printed in blacks, browns, and whites with patterns; and printed **kanga** (body wraps), worn by women in East Africa.

Fit for a King

Kente cloth is woven in narrow strips and brilliant colors and patterns. It was originally made by the Ashanti people (now in Ghana) for their kings, but it became popular with fashionable people throughout West Africa. Each color has a special meaning. Gold stands for high rank, green represents rebirth, red symbolizes power and passion, blue is believed to bring harmony, and yellow means fertility. Black is thought to be the color of seriousness and spirituality.

An official from Ghana wears a fine, locally woven kente cloth. The cloth is still worn today by Ashanti people.

Power and Prestige

In West Africa, two popular men's styles of draping cloth were *kyere w'anantu* ("show your legs"), in which cloth was wrapped around the body from the shoulders to the knees; and *okatakyie* ("brave man"), which covered the body from chest to calf and featured a long length of cloth draped over one arm. The first style was favored by strong, active, athletic men who wished to show off their bodies. The second, which looked dignified and impressive, was usually worn by chiefs. Women draped cloth to create skirts, shawls, and elaborate **geles** (head ties). The larger and more complicated the head tie, the higher the woman's status.

A Nigerian woman wears a head tie.

How did mud cloth get its name?

Fashions from Overseas

In the seventeenth and eighteenth centuries, European traders introduced new, brightly patterned batik cloth made from a wax-resistant dyeing process. Batik was originally made in Asia, but it was copied and mass-produced in Europe for export to Africa. Traders from Europe and Asia also introduced new clothing styles based on tunic robes or shirts and pants. Both became fashionable, especially in West Africa, and were copied and changed by African artisans to suit local tastes and conditions.

Nigerian men, dressed in bright tunic robes and hats, play traditional Hausa instruments.

Early Americas

The vast continents of North and South America were home to many different peoples. All had their own traditions of dress and their own special fashions and finery, but truly fine clothes were strictly limited to rich, powerful people.

Funeral Finery

In South America, when important people died, they were usually dressed in fine clothes and jewelry. They were then wrapped in "mummy-bundles" of specially woven blankets or **ponchos**, which are cloth cloaks with a central hole for the head. They were then placed in caves or buried underground. In some cultures, such as the Incas of the Andes Mountains, children who were killed as sacrifices to mountain gods were dressed in finery like mummies.

This mummified head from Nazca, Peru, is from about 200 B.C.

Feather Fashions

Among the Aztec people who lived in Mesoamerica, embroidered clothes and feather headdresses were top fashions for wealthy noblemen. Rich women wore embroidered clothes as well. The finest feathers were collected as tribute from conquered peoples or traded with rain-forest hunters and were treasured almost like gold. Lower grade feathers were also treasured. Feathers were woven into cloaks to create mobile, three-dimensional patterns, made into graceful handheld fans, or glued onto warriors' shields. The Aztecs thought feathers gave magical protection.

In this painting, Aztec emperor Montezuma (died 1521) wears an Aztec headdress.

Caddo and Choctaw Indians play *baggataway*, now known as lacrosse.

Sporting Gear

In many past civilizations, sports were a way of settling disputes between neighboring communities. Sports were cheaper, quicker, and less destructive than war. Games might last all day — or longer — with hundreds of men in each team. To take part, team members put on special finery. Typically, this included necklaces, body paint, decorative belts, and "tails" made of colored horsehair. These sport fashions showed which team players belonged to and may also have been thought to give players good luck, speed, and strength.

> **Which ancient sport was called the "Little Brother of War"?**

Colonial Clothes

At first, for religious and practical reasons, fashions in North America differed between colonies. In northern colonies, people preferred plain, simple clothing, and frivolous, "ungodly" fashions were banned. Cold weather also made thick, stiff, heavy clothes necessary for survival. Farther south, where the weather was warmer and religious attitudes were more relaxed, clothes were lighter and more elaborate. After about 1700, these differences disappeared, as rich colonists all chose to follow the latest European fashions. In the earlier part of the eighteenth century, European styles were very elaborate, but they became more sober toward the end of the century. The chief contrasts in clothing were between stylish town dwellers and roughly dressed country people.

George Washington displays stylish, rich clothes.

Europe 1500 – 1750

After 1500, Europe changed fast. New contacts with the Americas and with Asia brought new riches and materials from trade. These contacts also brought new ideas in art, literature, politics, and religion. Many of these new ideas and materials influenced European clothing styles.

Silk and Damask

By about 1500, Italy was the European center of fashion. Popes and Italian noble families ruled over brilliant courts. These rich, powerful Italians wore garments of silk or damask, which is a rich patterned fabric of cotton, linen, silk, or wool, imported from Asia. Noblemen wore new, short, fitted tunics, with close-fitting cloth stockings that were topped by open-fronted robes. Noblewomen wore gowns with low, square necks.

Queen Elizabeth I of England dances, wearing a robe with a long, tight "stomacher" bodice and a wide ruff.

Spanish Fashions

By about 1530, the gold from colonies in South America made Spain the wealthiest and most fashionable nation in Europe. Spanish fashions were copied throughout the European continent. Women's gowns had padded, bell-shaped skirts and stiff, boned bodices that were laced and worn like vests over blouses.

Men's styles featured short, tight, padded doublets, baggy **breeches**, and knitted silk stockings.

Guidubaldo II della Rovere, Duke of Urbino (1529-92), displays Spanish fashions.

King Charles I of England and his wife, French princess Henrietta Maria, both wear lace collars.

Soft and Natural

After about 1620, European fashions changed. Styles were softer, without padding, and followed the natural shape of the body. The Netherlands led fashion trends, so many designs featured costly, delicate, Netherlands-made lace. Men dressed in long jackets and knee-length breeches of silk or fine wool with ribbon trimming at the knees. Fashionable women wore gowns with natural waistlines, full, long skirts, high necklines, and wide collars. Underneath these fashions, men and women wore fine linen **chemises** (loose, skirt-like undergarments). Fashionable hairstyles were long, loose, and curled.

How long did the new French styles stay in fashion?

French Revolution

In about 1665, tailors in France introduced a revolutionary new fashion. For the first time, men wore three-piece outfits, called "**habits**," or suits, in matching fabrics. Each suit had a knee-length, open-fronted coat, close-fitting **waistcoat**, and breeches. The suit was worn with a shirt, a cravat (lightweight scarf), a three-corned hat, high-heeled shoes, and a heavy wig. After about 1670, women's robes had low necklines, **corsets** at the waist, stiffened bodices, and skirts open at the front to reveal decorative **petticoats**, which are women's slips or underskirts.

King Louis XIV of France (reigned 1643–1715) is wearing a very elegant suit.

21

Western World 1750 – 1900

During the nineteenth century, fashions changed more quickly than ever before, and fashionable styles were more elaborate. New businesses and industries created a new class of people with both money to spend on lavish clothes and opportunities for wearing them.

Napoleon's empress, Josephine, wears a dress inspired by ancient Greek fashion.

Greek Revival

In the late eighteenth century, new political ideas based on ancient Greek democracy became fashionable in North America and France. Greece also inspired new women's fashions. Between 1790 and 1815, fashionable dresses were long with high waists but no other shaping. For evening, they were made of thin white cotton to look like the **drapery** on Greeks statues. Modest women wore these dresses over flesh-colored underpants, but ultra-fashionable women also wore one petticoat underneath.

Corsets and Crinolines

Beginning in about 1820, dresses with corsetted bodices, wide skirts, and full sleeves became the new female fashion. They were worn with shawls and face-covering bonnets, plus layers of petticoats. By the 1850s, due to new technology, fashions changed again. Scientists created bright, permanent, aniline dyes. Engineers made

A lady from the Victorian era wears a tight corset.

steel springs for corsets and **crinolines** or huge **hoop** petticoats. For men, pants were paired with knee-length **frock coats** or heavy overcoats.

Dress Reform

Crinolines, corsets, and bustles — all frames worn with dresses to give them shape — were not very practical. Even at the time, they were criticized. In the 1850s, women's-rights activist Amelia Bloomer wore a new fashion designed by Elizabeth Smith Miller — baggy pants under full, knee-length skirts. Miller's invention, nicknamed "bloomers," did not became popular. In the 1890s, however, these women's pants were introduced again as women began to ride newly invented bicycles.

Few women wore bloomers.

What was a "Grecian bend"?

Just for Decoration

Between 1875 and 1900, fashionable women dressed in amazingly complicated styles. All were designed for good looks, not for comfort. Most were impossible to work in, so they were symbols of wealth and luxury. Some had **trains**, or trailing fabric, at the back. Some had yards of elaborate drapery. In the 1880s, tight, straight, tie-back skirts made walking difficult, and shawl-like dolman sleeves made it hard to move the arms. Hems, collars, cuffs, seams, and lapels were all trimmed with frills, braid, or embroidery. New men's fashions were much more comfortable — except for their stiff shirt collars. Men wore relaxed jackets for evening wear (called tuxedos in the United States) and roomy knickerbockers (knee breeches) plus tweed jackets for the country.

The dress of the bustle period covered a woman's body, from the waist down, in numerous ruffles and pleats. Such dresses were often dyed bright colors with the new aniline dyes.

Western World 1900 – 1950

At the start of the twentieth century, fashions were similar to the late nineteenth century. Then wars, social problems, and new ideas about politics, science, and art all had an impact on fashion. In less than twenty years, the clothes people wore changed dramatically.

In this 1905 Jewish community, the women wear long, frilly dresses.

Formal and Frilly

Until about 1910, men's fashions were somber and women's clothes were elaborate. For day, stylish men wore black frock coats and gray pants or a business suit with a matching jacket, pants, and waistcoat. For social evenings, men wore black pants with tail coats or tuxedos. Women wore long dresses with bloused bodices, full skirts, and tiny waists. Their necklines were high for daytime but low for evening wear. Corsets stiffened with whalebone helped create a woman's fashionable figure.

Bright Young Things

Millions of people died during World War I (1914-1918). As well as mourning the dead, those who survived were determined to change society and to enjoy themselves. They went on protest marches, admired new, abstract art, and danced to shocking new music: jazz. Women cut their hair, threw away their corsets, and wore short, simple skirts that ended just below the knee. The fashionable 1920s female figure was young, fit, and boyish.

This stylish couple is dancing the Charleston, a fashionable dance of the 1920s.

Elegance Again

In the 1920s and 1930s, business suits, tweed sports jackets, and gray wool pants became usual daywear for men. Pants now had cuffs, and the legs were much wider. The most fashionable, known as "Oxford Bags," measured 20 inches 51 cm) wide at the hem. Long, baggy breeches, called "Plus Fours" were also popular. They were worn with sleeveless, hand-knitted pullovers in "Fair-Isle'" designs, knitted in bands of patterns such as crosses, diamonds, and stars from two colors of wool. Fashions for women were elegant and ladylike.

By 1930, tuxedos were fashionable for dances and parties. Women's evening clothes were long again.

c. 1900 – 1950

Wartime Styles

From 1939 to 1945, World War II raged. For the first time, large numbers of women joined the armed forces in Europe and the United States. Most of the time, enlisted men and women wore uniforms. Civilian women's styles also looked like uniforms, with tight, neat jackets, short, straight skirts, and heavy, sensible shoes. For the first time, fashions included pants designed for women. Men's fashions were also practical and inspired by war. They included long, belted trench coats, tailored from waterproof fabric, and short, hooded **duffel coats** made of thick, warm, woolen cloth.

These British survived an air raid in 1942.

Western World 1950 – 2000

After the years of death and destruction caused by World War II, 1950s fashions brought back glamour. In the 1960s, fashion trends changed again. New styles, designed by and made for young people, led to a fashion revolution.

This 1952 full "New Look" skirt from Paris was shaped with layers of petticoats.

The New Look

In 1947, French designer Christian Dior introduced his latest haute couture collection. It caused a sensation! Soon nicknamed the "New Look," it featured full skirts, tight waists, low necklines, high heels, and feminine, curving outlines. The New Look was a dramatic contrast to wartime uniform styles and remained popular for years. Expensive and impractical for everyday wear, the New Look was most frequently worn by wealthy people.

Mini, Midi, Maxi

In 1965, young designers Mary Quant, from Britain, and André Courrèges, from France, made the world's first miniskirts. Styled as part of simple, shapeless, shift dresses, mini hemlines varied in length but all were high above the knee. Miniskirts became immensely fashionable. They were worn with stylish shoes or boots and nylon tights, or pantyhose, another 1960s invention. By 1970, new, calf-length (midi) and floor-length (maxi) skirts became fashionable.

Thin British supermodel "Twiggy" wears a miniskirt in 1965.

Baby Boomers

The baby boomer generation (people who were born between 1946 and 1964) became a strong fashion influence beginning in the 1950s. They rebelled against the bland fashion of their parents. In the 1950s, many boys wore leather jackets and jeans, copying film stars such as Marlon Brando, while girls wore tight shirts, slim skirts, and stiletto heels. Male beatniks wore black sweaters and chinos, while girls wore straight skirts, black leotards, and sandals or ballet slippers. In the 1960s and 1970s, dazzling **pyschedelic** (colorful, wildly patterned) styles were popular, as were **hippy kaftans** (full-length garments with long sleeves). In the 1970s and 1980s, punk fashions with studs and zippers became popular, as did Goth styles, which feature black clothing and hair dyed black.

This 1960's shirt is an example of the "flower power" style.

1950 – 2000

Which automobile took its name from a 1960s fashion?

Power Dressing and 1990s Fashion

In the 1980s, new political ideas and values inspired a new style known as Power Dressing. Men and women **yuppies** (Young Urban Professionals) aimed for high-flying careers and hoped to make lots of money. Men wore dark, tailored suits, expensive shoes, shirts and ties, and pants held up by red suspenders. Women wore straight, knee-length skirts and jackets with wide-padded shoulders. In the 1990s, young people tried a more urban, casual look. Loose pants and sportswear were popular, as were expensive designer clothes, including jeans that cost hundreds of dollars made by firms such as Calvin Klein and Guess.

A fashion model wears a shirt with shoulder pads and white slacks during a 1980s fashion show.

Global Styles Today

Fashion is always changing. Fashionable shapes, styles, designs, and decorations vary from place to place and age to age. They all serve the same purpose. They offer people a way to tell others who they are through what they wear.

Today, fashion designers will often go to extremes to try to create a new look.

Global Couture

Many new fashions are still created by trendsetting designers. Today, however, modern manufacturing, shipping, and advertising techniques mean that millions of copies can be made and sold all around the world. News of the latest styles can now be sent around the world in seconds, using the Internet, satellite TV, or cell phones. As in the past, only a few very rich men and women can afford actual haute couture originals.

Actresses such as Sienna Miller promote fashion at public events.

Entertainers

Modern communications also mean that fashion has become closely linked to the entertainment industry. New styles are created by top performers and copied by their fans. Manufacturers and designers also ask celebrities to appear in public wearing their clothes. They know that the media attention this attracts is far more effective than costly advertising.

Culture Combinations

Global communications and manufacturing have also created fashionable new styles. These are based on a combination of ancient local traditions and Western styles, including haute couture. In China, India, and Africa, local designers often use beautiful local fabrics, colors, and techniques to add flair to basic Western garments, such as jackets or skirts. Western designers, for their part, often look to foreign cultures to find new patterns and inspiration.

This modern "street" fashion, made by an independent designer, combines Western and Asian designs.

How do haute couture designers make most of their money today?

Cheap Style, Street Style

Twenty-first-century fashion is different from fashions that have been worn before. Independent designers create their own looks and can sell them in boutiques and on their own Web sites. Teenagers create their own fashion trends, which often get picked up by designers. If enough people choose a look, whether it is haute couture or street style, it is fashionable.

CLEARANCE

Take an additional

50% off

Markdown taken at register

Today, fashionable clothes are accessible for most people and can often be bought at low prices.

Glossary

bogolan West African cloth printed with patterns using mud

batik a method of dyeing a fabric by protecting parts of it from the dye with wax

bodice a woman's laced outer garment

breeches pants that end above the knee

bustle a frame used to expand the fullness of the back of a woman's skirt

chemises women's loose, skirt-like undergarments

chitons tunics worn in ancient Greece

choli a close-fitting blouse, worn in India

corsets in medieval times, outer garments worn to shape the waist, hips, and bust. In later times, corsets were typically worn beneath dresses.

crinolines hoop-shaped petticoat stiffened with steel wire

diadems headbands or crowns, originally worn by royalty

dhotis loincloths, or lengths of cloth wrapped around the lower body, worn by men in India

doublets close-fitting tunics, worn in Europe in the late Middle Ages and again in the sixteenth century

drapery clothing styled in loose folds

duffel coats hooded overcoats made of thick woolen cloth, fastened with toggles

emblems visual symbols or badges

etu West African fabric dyed dark blue with indigo

farji close-fitting coat, worn first in ancient Persia

formal organized, controlled, polite, or dressed up, as for a special occasion

frock coats knee-length coats for men, often double-breasted

geles head wraps, worn by women in West Africa

ghaghra a full skirt with sewn side seams, worn in India

habits sets of clothes, worn in seventeenth- and eighteenth-century France

haute couture "high fashion;" expensive, exclusive styles

heraldic decorated with patterns showing membership of a noble family or loyalty to a lord

himation cloak worn in ancient Greece

hippy young person who rebelled against social customs in the 1960s and 1970s and who called for love, peace, and freedom and opposed war

hoop dome-shaped petticoat, strengthened with whalebone rods

hose stockings made of woven fabric

isar wide, baggy pants, first worn in ancient Persia

jamah close-fitting coat, worn in ancient Persia.

kaftan long, close-fitting robe, first worn in Central Asia

kanga length of cloth wrapped around the body, worn in East Africa

kente cloth West African cloth woven in narrow strips and then sewn together

linen fabric made from the flax plant

peer equal in terms of age or social class

petticoats women's slips or underskirts

peploses robes with double layers of fabric for the bodices, worn by women in ancient Greece

ponchos cloaks like blankets with a narrow slit in the middle to put the head through, worn in South America

prestige high status

psychedelic colorful, distorted, surreal visual effects such as those caused by mind-changing substances

saris Indian dresses made of single lengths of cloth wrapped around the body

scarification decorative pattern of scars made by cutting the skin

shamans people who are seen as the magical or spiritual healers for their communities

silk a fine, lustrous material made from the unwound threads of silk worm cocoons

tebenna semi-circular robe worn by Etruscans in Italy

toga semi-circular cloak worn by citizens in ancient Rome

trains trailing fabric at the back of a skirt

waistcoat a short, sleeveless, collarless garment worn mostly by men

yuppies "Young Urban Professionals;" a nickname for young people working in high-status city jobs

Answers

Page 5: pronounced *oat coot-yoor,* it is French for "high fashion"

Page 7: a Frenchwoman, about 1750

Page 9: an essential symbol of royal power, false beards were tied on by both young male and woman pharaohs

Page 11: After about 50 B.C., Rome began to conquer northern European lands. Wigs made from blond or bleached hair, cut from northern captives, started a new fashion.

Page 13: gold and fur

Page 14: dragons symbolized the emperor's power and also the heavens above the Earth

Page 17: its designs were printed using colored earths and other natural dyes

Page 19: the game known as lacrosse, which got its French name from European settlers

Page 21: for hundreds of years

Page 23: a fashionable female shape in about 1860. Skirts were tied into a big bunch at the back and supported by a bustle.

Page 25: Tuxedo Park, which was an exclusive district in New York State where many fashionable people lived

Page 27: the minicar, first made by British in the 1960s, named after the miniskirt

Page 29: by selling perfumes and makeup or letting their brand names be used to advertise mass-market clothes

Index